Strawberry Shortcake

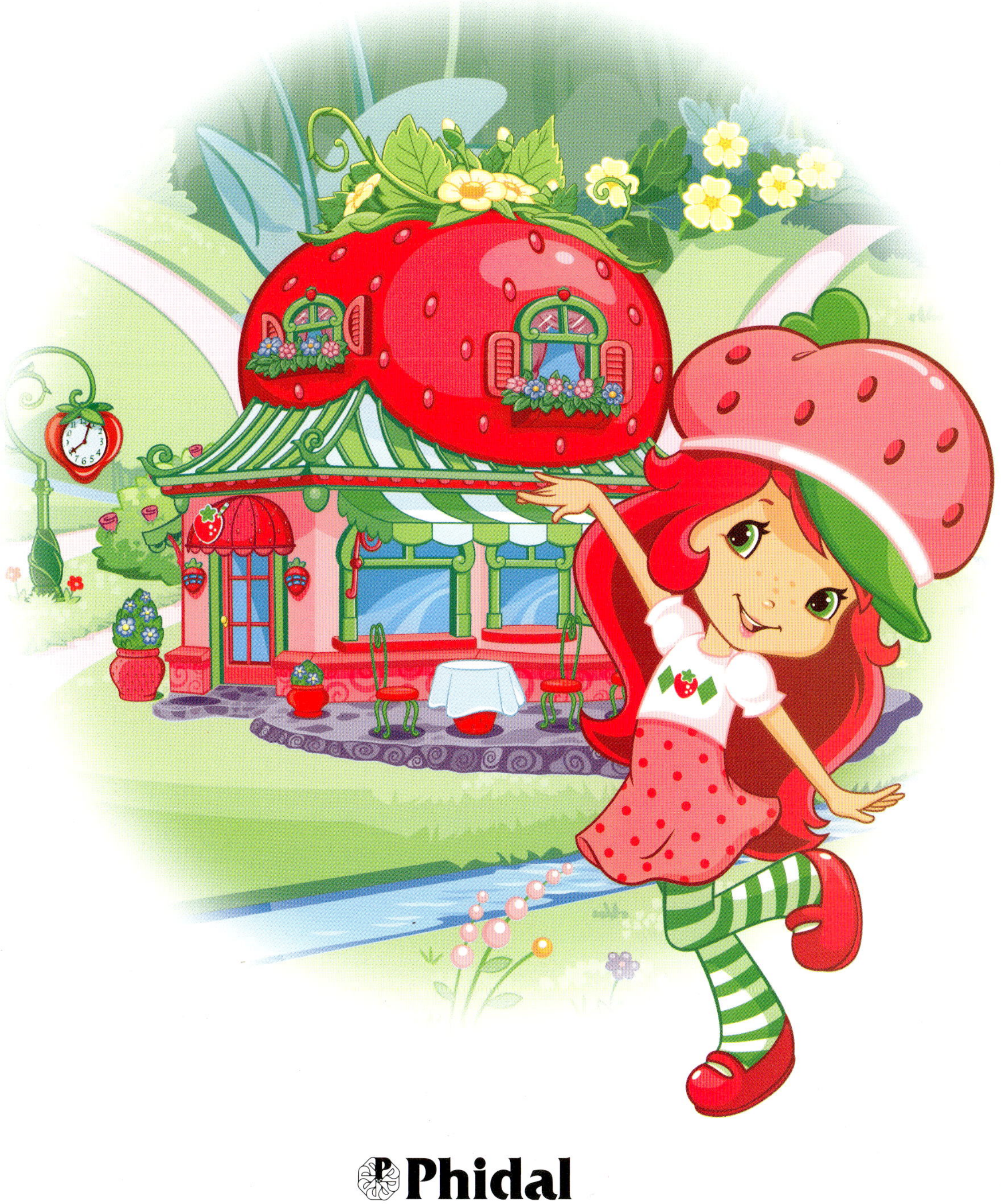

Phidal

Berry Bitty Friends

These girls are a berry friendly bunch! Place your stickers over the shadows in the color circles with the right girl's name.

Tutti Frutti Cuties!

Every girl is one of a kind, and they each have a signature fruit to prove it! Can you tell which fruit is each girl's favorite? Use your stickers.

Summer Sweetness

Life's a bowl of berries, and no one knows that better than Strawberry Shortcake and her friends! Decorate the scene with your stickers.

Fruitastic Fun

Strawberry Shortcake is thirsty for some fun! Using your stickers, can you help her count the items and complete the groups below?

Smoothie-licious

Can you tell what Strawberry Shortcake is sipping? Here's a hint: it's berry juicy!
Fill in the blank spots with your stickers to complete the scene.

Home Sweet Home

What a sweet spot! Strawberry Shortcake's home looks pretty as punch! Place your stickers in the right blank spots.

A Drop of Delicious

Strawberry Shortcake is serving Lemon Meringue some freshly-squeezed pink lemonade. Use your stickers to make the scene below look like the one above.

Lemon Meringue

Pretty as Punch

Lemon Meringue and her friends are wearing some tutti-cutie outfits! Place your stickers over the shadows next to the right color combinations to see who is wearing what.

3

Berry-licious Patterns

The berry bitty girls are lining up for some fruitastic fun!
Complete the patterns in each row using your stickers.

4

Sweet Salon
Lemon Meringue's lovely Lemon Salon is a drop of deliciousness!
Decorate the sweet scene with your stickers.

Berrykins

Orange Blossom, Raspberry Torte, and all the berry girls have matching Berrykins! Match up each Berrykin with their berry special girl.

Fruity Formulas

These fresh and delicious ingredients equal sweet and tasty fruitastic fun!
Use your stickers to complete each row below.

Surf, Sand, and Sun!

The berry bitty girls are having some sweet summer fun at the beach. How many of each item can you find? Place your number stickers in the right circles.

Sweet and Tasty

This perfect punch is packed with the sweetness of summer! What ingredients make it so fruitilicious? Place your stickers over the shadows to find out.

Raspberry Torte

Berry Bedazzling

Strawberry Shortcake's dress is simply lovely! Can you tell what's missing from the scene? Fill in the blanks with your stickers.

Fashionable Formulas

Look at the fruity fashion items below and solve the equations in each row with the help of your stickers.

Fresh Fashions Boutique

Raspberry Torte's chic boutique is a real gem! Decorate the scene with your stickers.

Sweet Series

Look at all the fruitastic items! Use your stickers to help Orange Blossom, Strawberry Shortcake, and Raspberry Torte complete the patterns in each row.

12

Fresh, Fruity Fashion

The berry girls have each designed their very own sweet chic purses! Can you tell whose handbag belongs to whom? Place your stickers over the shadows.

Perfectly Sweet Patterns

Strawberry Shortcake knows that sweet is always in style! Can you tell which of your stickers match the berry pretty patterns?

Berry Bright Day

Raspberry Torte and Strawberry Shortcake are having a berry blast together. With your stickers, make the bottom scene look like the one above.

Blueberry Muffin

Berry Sparkly

Strawberry Shortcake and the berry girls are shining with glitz and glam! Use your stickers to fill in the blank spots and complete the pattern in each row.

Berry Sweet Music

The berry girls know how to follow their own beats to make life sweet! Find out who plays which instrument by matching your stickers to the shadows below.

Berry Bitty City

Berry Bitty City is a simply lovely place to live! Decorate the scene with your stickers.

Fashion Fun

These pretty hip berry girls are each wearing super stylish headbands! Use your stickers to match the right headband to each girl.

Piano Pooch

Pupcake is playing some sweet beats. Fill in the missing spots to complete the scene with the help of your stickers.

Dazzling Equations

The berry girls know it's important to always be true to the music in you and reach for the stars! Using your stickers, solve the sparkly equations in each row.

Groove-alicious

Music is what friendship sounds like! Make the bottom scene look like the one on top with your stickers.